CLASSIC CARS
AN IMAGINATION LIBRARY SERIES

THE STORY OF

Jaguar

by Jim Mezzanotte

GARETH**STEVENS**
PUBLISHING
A WRC Media Company

Please visit our web site at: www.garethstevens.com
For a free color catalog describing Gareth Stevens Publishing's
list of high-quality books and multimedia programs,
call 1-800-542-2595 (USA) or 1-800-387-3178 (Canada).
Gareth Stevens Publishing's fax: (414) 332-3567.

Library of Congress Cataloging-in-Publication Data

Mezzanotte, Jim.
    The story of Jaguar / by Jim Mezzanotte.
        p. cm. — (Classic cars: an imagination library series)
    Includes bibliographical references and index.
    ISBN 0-8368-4535-8 (lib. bdg.)
    1. Jaguar automobile—History—Juvenile literature. I. Title. II. Series.
TL215.J3M48   2005
629.222'2—dc22   2004059104

First published in 2005 by
Gareth Stevens Publishing
A WRC Media Company
330 West Olive Street, Suite 100
Milwaukee, WI 53212 USA

Text: Jim Mezzanotte
Cover design and page layout: Scott M. Krall
Series editors: JoAnn Early Macken and Mark J. Sachner
Picture Researcher: Diane Laska-Swanke

Photo credits: Cover, pp. 5, 7, 11, 17, 19 © Ron Kimball; pp. 9, 13, 15, 21 © National Motor Museum

Printed in the United States of America

1 2 3 4 5 6 7 8 9 09 08 07 06 05

Front cover: **Since the 1930s, Jaguar cars have been famous for their speed, power, and beauty.**

TABLE OF CONTENTS

Words that appear in the glossary are printed in **boldface** type the first time they occur in the text.

HIGH SPEED

Jaguar is a car company in England. It is named after a fast, wild cat. It makes fast cars. The SS100 was an early Jaguar sports car. It came out in 1935. The car got its name from its top speed. It could go 100 miles (160 kilometers) per hour. Back then, not many cars could go so fast.

The SS100 was long and low. It had swooping fenders and big headlights. The car did not have a lot of room. It had a bumpy ride. But it was fun to drive, especially with the top down!

Compared to today's cars, this 1938 SS100 may seem old-fashioned. At the time, however, it was one of the most exciting sports cars around.

SPECIAL CARS

After World War II, Jaguar made a new sports car. It was called the XK120. The car had a strong, powerful engine. It was even faster than the SS100. It could go 120 miles (193 km) per hour. The car had a modern look. People loved it!

In the 1950s, Jaguar sports cars became famous. They were fast and beautiful. Many were **exported** to the United States. Some were **coupes**, and some were **convertibles**. When Jaguars went by, people stopped to stare. Jaguars were very special cars.

This Jaguar is a 1956 XK140. It is an improved version of the XK120. Many people dreamed of owning a Jaguar sports car.

A WINNING STREAK

Jaguar also built racing cars. In the 1950s, these cars were very successful. They won many times at the 24 Hours of Le Mans. This race is held in France. At Le Mans, cars have to race for twenty-four hours! It is hard to race for such a long time. Many cars break down before the finish line.

For racing, Jaguar built the C-Type. It was similar to an XK120. The C-Type won twice at Le Mans. Then Jaguar built a new racing car. It was called the D-Type. This car won Le Mans three years in a row. For a while, nobody could beat Jaguar!

A race car driver zooms past a crowd in a 1956 Jaguar D-type. In the 1950s, the D-type became famous for winning races.

THE CLASSIC CAT

In 1961, the Jaguar E-Type came out. It was long and low. The body had a lot of curves. The car almost looked like a big cat! Many E-Types were sold in the United States. In the United States, the E-Type was called the XKE. It was a very popular car. It was the most famous Jaguar of all time.

The E-Type started out as a race car. It was supposed to replace the D-Type. Then Jaguar made it into a regular sports car. It had a powerful engine. It also had excellent brakes and **suspension**. The E-Type was a **bargain**. It was similar to sports cars that cost a lot more money.

The XKE was a big hit in the United States. People were amazed by the car's beauty and speed. This XKE is a 1964 convertible.

THE LAST E-TYPE

By the 1970s, cars had changed. The United States had car **regulations**. Cars had to be safer. They had to make less **pollution**. The E-Type changed. The engine made less pollution. But it had less power, too.

The company put a new engine in the car. The old engine had six **cylinders**. The new engine had twelve cylinders. It was a V-12 engine. It was in the shape of a "V." Not many cars used a big V-12 engine!

The E-Type had been around for a long time. Jaguar decided to stop making it. The last E-Type was built in 1974.

This 1972 E-type has a V-12 engine for smooth power. At the time, E-types were still great sports cars. But they would not be made much longer.

ROOM FOR PASSENGERS

Jaguar did not just make sports cars. The company also made luxury **sedans**. These cars were big and comfortable. They had a smooth ride. After Jaguar stopped making the E-Type, it kept making sedans. The cars had six-cylinder engines or V-12 engines.

These cars do not look as exciting as the sports cars. But don't let their looks fool you! The cars have the same kind of engines, brakes, and suspension. They are fun to drive. A Jaguar sedan might not look fast, but it is!

Several people can ride in this Jaguar XJ6 sedan. This model has a powerful six-cylinder engine. The car is comfortable, but it is also fast.

SHOWING OFF

Many Jaguar owners are crazy about their cars! They join Jaguar clubs so they can get together with other Jaguar owners. These people take their Jaguars on special trips. They even race their Jaguars. Some Jaguar owners also enter their cars in special shows.

In these shows, cars win prizes for being in the best condition. Everything is cleaned and polished. Even the engine area is very clean. Some Jaguar owners **restore** their Jaguars. They take the cars apart, down to the last nut and bolt. Then they rebuild the cars, so they look brand new. A restored Jaguar looks like it just left the showroom!

This 1964 XKE coupe has been restored. Although the car was built more than forty years ago, it looks brand new.

THE FASTEST JAGUAR

In the 1990s, Jaguar built a special sports car. It was called the XJ220. It could reach a top speed of more than 200 miles (320 kilometers) per hour! It is the fastest Jaguar ever made. For a while, it was the fastest sports car in the world.

The XJ220 is a **mid-engine** car. The engine is behind the seats. With the engine in the middle, the car handles very well. The engine has **turbochargers**. It is very powerful. The XJ220 is big, but it is also light. The body is made of **aluminum**. Jaguar built fewer than three hundred of these cars. They are very expensive!

In the Jaguar XJ220, the driver sits ahead of the engine. This car is much faster than most other cars. Driving it at high speeds takes a lot of skill.

Today, Jaguar makes a new sports car. It is called the XK8. The car looks a lot like the old E-type. It has a long, low hood and many curves. The XK8 has a powerful V-8 engine. This engine has eight cylinders. It is in the shape of a "V" like the V-12. It is made of aluminum to keep down weight.

Jaguar makes a special version of this car. It is called the XKR. On the outside, the XKR looks a lot like the XK8. But the engine in this car is more powerful. The XKR is one fast cat!

Books (Nonfiction)	*Jaguar. Ultimate Cars* (series). A. T. McKenna (Abdo & Daughters Publishing)
	Jaguars. High Performance (series). Michael Green (Capstone Press)
	The Ultimate Classic Car Book. Quentin Willson (DK Publishing)

Videos (Nonfiction)	*Jaguar E-Type.* (A&E Home Video)
	The Jaguar E-Type Experience. (Kultur Video)
	Jaguar XJ220: The Official Story. (Kultur Video)
	The Visual History of Cars: Jaguar. (MPI Home Video)

PLACES TO WRITE AND VISIT

Here are three places to contact for more information:

Jaguar Daimler Heritage Trust Museum
Browns Lane
Allesley, Coventry
CV5 9DR, England
44-2476-203322
www.jaguarcars.com/uk/ jdht/searchform.cgi?start

Petersen Automotive Museum
6060 Wilshire Blvd.
Los Angeles, CA 90036
USA
1-323-930-2277
www.petersen.org

The Welsh Classic Car Museum
223 North 5th Street
P.O. Box 4130
Steubenville, OH 43952
USA
www.welshent.com/ museum.htm

WEB SITES

Web sites change frequently, but we believe the following web sites are going to last. You can also use good search engines, such as **Yahooligans!** [www.yahooligans.com] or **Google** [www.google.com], to find more information about Jaguar. Here are some keywords to help you: *British sports cars, C-Type, D-Type, E-Type, Jaguar, Le Mans, SS100, XJ220, XJ series, XK8, XKE,* and *XK series.*

www.catdriver.com/gallery/
This web site is hosted by the Jaguar Club of Florida. You can click on photo galleries for many different car shows, with pictures of Jaguars and other British cars.

www.classic-british-cars.com/jaguar-cars-home.html
Visit this web site to view pictures of many different Jaguar models, from the SS100 to the XJ220.

www.classicargarage.nl/english/frames/index2.htm
At this web site, you can view wonderful images of different Jaguar models.

www.classiccarshop.co.uk/classic_jaguar.htm
This British web site has many Jaguars for sale. Visit this site to see some nice Jaguar pictures, including views of engines and interiors.

www.etypejag.com
At this web site, you can learn all about the Jaguar E-Type. Visit this site for a history of the E-type and many pictures of E-types, including ones that are being restored.

www.jag-lovers.org/snaps/
This web site has hundreds of pictures of Jaguars, provided by Jaguar lovers all over the world!

www.jaguarusa.com/us/en/home.htm
Visit this official Jaguar web site for pictures of all the latest Jaguar models and information about them, too.

www.seattlejagclub.org/jpics.html
At this web site, you can find pictures and histories of many different Jaguar models.

GLOSSARY

You can find these words on the pages listed. Reading a word in a sentence helps you understand it even better.

aluminum (uh-LUME-in-um) — a light-weight metal. 18, 20

bargain (BAR-gun) — something that is valuable but has a low price. 10

convertibles (kun-VER-tuh-bulls) — cars with a top that can be folded down or removed. 6, 10

coupes (KOOPS) — cars with a hard top and two doors. 6, 16, 20

cylinders (SIL-in-durz) — tubes inside an engine where gas explodes, giving the engine power. 12, 14, 20

exported (EX-por-ted) — sent to other countries to be sold. 6

mid-engine (MYD-en-jin) — having the engine in the middle, behind the seats and ahead of the rear wheels. 18

pollution (puh-LOO-shun) — man-made waste that harms people and the environment. 12

regulations (reg-you-LAY-shunz) — laws or rules that require people to do things a certain way. 12

restore (ree-STOR) — bring back to original condition. 16

sedans (seh-DANZ) — cars with hard tops and room for four or more people. 14

suspension (suh-SPEN-shun) — the parts that connect the wheels to a car and help the car go smoothly over bumps. 10, 14

turbochargers (TUR-boe-char-jurz) — devices that force more air into an engine, giving it more power. 18

INDEX